Colours of Poetry
IX

CONTEMPLATE THE NOW

by
Colin Michael

Cover Painting by Colin Michael

ISBN: 9798710071007
Imprint: Independently published
Colours of Poetry IX by Colin Michael 2021

Contents

I see the printed word as a form of visual theory that explains a lot yet holds back a hidden context to what the possible meaning could be. It enlightens, evokes passion and debates on all levels of thoughts and emotions. As we all know a word can mean a multitude of things but in the correct or incorrect set of words becomes something very different. Each to their own.

246

One's

One should always
question oneself

Whoever one is
That's one's mantra

Otherwise one
Could be misleadingly

Lead oneself into selflessness
Reliance on one's own

A disability to one's own self-belief
After all I am "the" one

One is not wrong there
Is one, one is, is not one.

247

Stand alone

I've been dreaming dreams
Of what used to be
Once you left me standing
Lonely as anyone can be
I felt abandoned inside myself
It's the best thing that happened

To me

I still have a thought of you
That I can never let go
Looking forward to new beginnings
It's exciting to remember
What was and what has been
It's the best thing that happened

To me

With an unburdened mindset
I open the doors to pastures new
To breath in pure clean air
Exhaling the smoke that choked
Clouding my train of thoughts
It's the best thing that happened

To me

248

No idea

I was

I did

I am

Was I

Did I

Am I

I could

I have

I will

Could I

Have I

Will I

Probably not.

249

Exposing my body

I am just standing in the rain
With pitter patter gentle drops
Falling off the green leaves above

They are bouncing down on my face
With a warm feeling running down
Soaking my white cotton shirt

That now clings exposing my body
With this refreshing feeling I relax
Under the umbrella of the trees

Waiting for the clouds to depart
Leaving me to resume my walk home
To a warm log fire and a cup of tea.

250

Basic instinct

Out of my head coming down
To a new level I never knew

Reach up to hold on to nothing
It's the best I can do for you

I need to disappear from it all
Hide away out of the grid

Every day needs not be the same
As I find out what's best to do

Following my basic instinct
Surviving out of reach of it all.

251

Ending twist

Don't thing badly of me
For I do not of you

Though I wonder
Where this is leading us to

With or without you
Leading you down this road

Of never ending twists and turns
Dramatic ups and down

The path chosen is not so clear
Though we shall be together

For ever.

252

Me or You

How come it's all about me

Again

I mean really it's about you

After all.

253

Just a thought

Roses are

RED,

Violence is

BLUE,

I've got a

GUN

I'm gonna shoot

YOU.

254

Ain't gonna

I guess you have wondered
Where I have been lately

I can tell you
Only if you would listen

That ain't going to happen
As you never did

Roll back those crocodile tears
Fake feeling of meaningful love

Lost on my sensibility of reality
Checks and balances all void

When all said and done
I guess it was just on a Post-it

That you picked up off the fridge
You must see how it's about to end.

255

For what begins

Everybody is trying to tell me
What's best for me

Nothing I can't handle
As there's nothing I haven't got

When you look into my heart
Only you know what's going on

Surrender your love to me
For what begins will never end

Or so the story is told
Over a warm fire glowing

I hold back the tears of joy
For I will never feel blue with you

Hold on to my hand so tight
I am the same boy I used to be.

256

Satisfying day

The cock crowed in the distance
As grandad nodded off peacefully
While the clattering plates were gathered

Just another Sunday lunch being prepared
With the sweet smell of cooked roast lamb
And the potatoes spat in duck fat lard

We gathered as a family round the table
Outside under the old oak tree umbrella
Grandfather awoke just on time

As the bottle of wine was uncorked
With a satisfaction resounding pop
The aroma of an aged Bordeaux red
A quick sniff of the cork and small taste

The food was placed on a large oval plate
Age before beauty as servicing ritual began
No argument just idle chatting consumed
A satisfying family Sunday was had by all.

257

Rubber ring

Life is a never ending beach
Ebbing and flowing
With the tide of time
It brings with it life

Even when you feel crabby
Lost all at sea
There is always a life line
A rubber ring to protect you

To bring you back
Safe to the shoreline
Though there are monsters
In the depths of the darkness

Waiting to bring you down
As you flounder in storms
That lash violently around
Leaving you exhausted washed up

No matter what is thrown at you
You will always float to the surface
Where you can breathe fresh air
To fill your body with life.

258

Never

A disorderly mindset with gravitas
Is surely the way to stay alive

In this climate of relentless change
Spiralling up into that black hole

A complexity to drain yourself of all
The respite will never come

Depart the terminus of no choice
With a genial drip drip of the tap

Swirling round and round only to sink
Down to join all others in that pool

Discord is a mindset of gravity
Pulling you to the abyss of never never

Never mind it will never come to that
But it will it has and it is here "the now".

259

So

It's all so different

After all I pay my rent

It's only a small tent

I am quite content

With what I spent

It's going to be lent

When I get to Ghent

Where it's so different

After all I have spent.

260

Monkey business

A monkey in a tree
Is looking at me
What does he see
Well it will be me

As I was about to say
Do you want to play
Later on that day
He hit his head on that tree

I thought this was strange
As though he was in a rage
It turned it was his age
Having turned over a new page

All in all it was not a monkey
Hanging around in a tree
It was me I had no key
And I needed to have a pee.

261

Wood

Blackbird singing in the pale moonlight
A lone fox sends out a chilling shrill at night
Leaves are crunched under foot
As the hunter stalks his weary way

A click of a camera shutter mirror opening
Capturing that fleeting moment in time
As badger cubs play outside the burrow
Mother digs deep broadening her furrow

The worm has turned heading home
With descending pitter patter drops of rains
Hitting the bare soil as a clap of thunder
Resonates from tree trunk to trunk

Woodland creatures dart this way and that
Taking refuge in nooks and crannies
Hidden for the most discerning beady eyes
All is quiet across the forest bar the rain.

262

Roundabout

I've been doing some thinking
After doing some drinking
Not to clear what it was about
Though there was this roundabout

I negotiated my exit plan B
Totally forgetting Plan A
After hitting a fallen tree
While drinking a warm cup of tea

A man stepped out into my path
Only to enrage my better half
Being thrown forward with a scream
Splitting her tub of deluxe ice cream

What was that all about
I said it's a new roundabout
Not too clear after the second beer
It was not a tree but a furry deer

I better get us home now
Clean up this messy thinking
That got me into confused drinking
After all what was it all about.

263

Bite me

A tinsy winsy spider
Climbed up my trouser leg
Biting my nether regions

I was in a terrible state

It was not the spider
That caused the great pain
It was me hitting myself
So terribly terribly hard

Down there you know where

The doctors looked puzzled
As he had a fondle a peek
Black and blue sorry son

It's all over for you.

264

Misinterpretation

The grey darkness was not my friend that day
Filling me with an uncontrollable desire to leave

Find a corner where I did not have to think
A place of solace tranquillity of peacefulness

A whirlpool of emotions descended over me
Filling me with anxieties I never knew

With a comforting thought it would end
Maybe not exactly how I wish it to cease

Reacting to our previous misinterpretation
Filling me with arguably painful regrets

I picked up my mobile to text a message
So sorry my darling I forgot our secret date.

265

New horizons

Every day is the same
When reality changes
With this perpetual distancing
Overriding your life

A one-way ticket to nowhere
Like tripping down a worm hole
Where nothing is ever the same
Lost in the vacuum of space

With the winds of change
Actually blowing your mind
Depriving you of needed oxygen
Eyes wide open grasping at light

Step back into a timeline of choice
See the positive aspects of change
Let all your senses open doors
New horizons a beacon of energy.

266

Pants

Shall I change

You should change

"Why"

Because you must

It's good to change

"It's not"

I read somewhere

That it's good to change

"You're sure"

But I am happy

Happy not to change

"No way"

It's for the best

What if I don't change

"What"

I like who I am

You are so ready to change

"Get out"

That's it

Let's both change

"Pants".

267

Virtual speed dating

Do you mind if I sit down next to you
Ask you a question about what you do

I am a simple man with not much to say
Well that's I what I think anyway

I found your profile on the world wide web
You seemed interacting I texted I am Ted

So here we are as it were in the flesh
Though it's virtual I don't want to sound fresh

Do I come up to your expectations
Am I not a handsome revelation

Your profile picture does it do you justice
More information as I am out of practice

This hologram it keeps breaking up
Is it your way of saying we are splitting up.

268

Goodbye

I left Africa with nothing

My soul had gone

It was ripped from me

I really had no idea why

A cruel twist of fate

Bestowed upon me

Tears that ran deep

Though no idea why

They just came

Dropping like rain

Hitting the ground

With a painful thud

Mother's faint whispers

England oh England

It meant nothing to me

As I said goodbye

To my favourite tree.

269

Spend wisely

Love is a passionate embrace
A moment worth savouring
Enjoying to share one another

A mayfly lives for a day
In that brief capsule of time
It lives loves and dies

Everyone can achieve
When you spend wisely
Tick tock every second

Nothing is lost for ever
Savour every dying moment
As though it was your last.

270

It's short

Time is not on my side

I have no time
What time is it
Do you have time
What time to meet

Let's slow time down

I have lots of time
How much time
Do I have to spend
How do I save time

Going backwards in time

I had plenty of time
To spend unwisely
To do as I wish with
To waste it wistfully

Time left me disconnected

I lay thinking of time
What could I do with it
Do hold on tightly
What if I let it go

It's time for you to decide.

271

Prevailing drift

Acceptance is a price you pay
To be creative in every way
Avoidance is a bridge to cross
Turbulent waters crashing beneath

Mind thoughts drift this way and that
In vain hope of clarity that may come
Distributed inner interventions pervading
With lawless diseased manipulation

Breathless anxieties haunting
Accounting every pebble on a beach
Uneven shades of many shapes
Never to be unturned never answered

With this constant convection
You grip the told narrative
Interpreting actual facts not fiction
Leading you to pay to be accepted.

272

Opportunity beckons

I had a sequential thought

That a train had arrived

On platform thirteen

Departure 20.21

Destination wherever

It would be driverless

A window of opportunity.

273

Unclean thoughts

I sat down on the bus 69

A man opposite looked at me

When do you get off

I thought for a moment

That's a bit personal

Why would he ask such a thing

After all it's a private matter

He repeated the question

My thoughts had been violated

I felt unclean and nervous

blurting out "same time everyday"

He looked disgustingly at me

That's going to cost you.

274

Ghoulish sounds

We made a tent out of bed sheets

Mum's broom to push the middle up

Inside teddy and I camped out for the night

We could hear all sorts of ghoulish sounds

That swelled around the darkness

Screams of owls from every direction

Someone is coming to attack teddy and I

Would be my sister the wicked witch

With evil books of strange words hogwash

Wind in the willows or Heathcliff

Whichever the witch would read them out

Just as teddy and I drifted off to noddy land

Then chomping footsteps a door creaking

A breach in the tent with hand of a demon

"Hot chocolate with homemade cookies"

With great reluctance the gifts were taken

Next time not so nice there will be trouble

Trouble at t'mill I think teddy...we sleep.

275

Cloud

We are all completely alone
That's the truth of it

Some of us are on cloud nine
Some of us are in the cloud

Whichever or wherever we are
We are nothing at all

Some of us see faces in the clouds
Some of us are flying in the clouds

Whichever we're nothing
That's the god damn truth

Some of us want to be on cloud nine
Some of us get high on the cloud

Whichever or whenever if you're happy
Create your own cloud fly high.

Biography

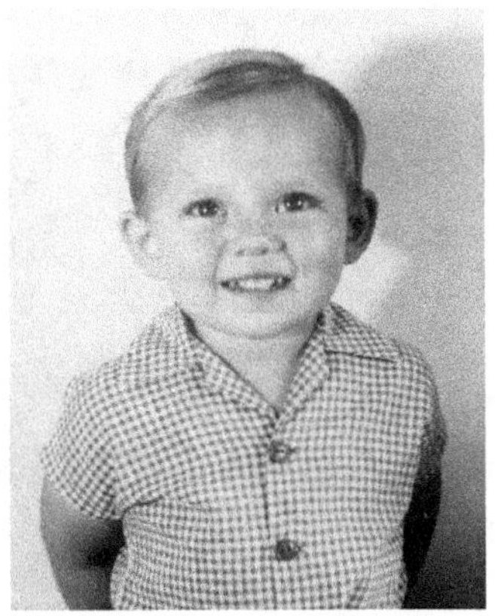

Colin Michael
Artist, Poet, YouTube Video maker

Born in Bulawayo in 1959
Lived in Salisbury (Harare), Southern Rhodesia
(Zimbabwe) 1959-66
Emigrated to London, England in 1966
Emigrated to Paris, France in 2018

Education
Alfred Beit School, Mabelreign, Southern Rhodesia
(Zimbabwe)
Middleton Rose Hill, Sutton, London
Boughton Monchelsea, Maidstone, Kent
Biggin Hill, Bromley, Kent
Churchill School, Westerham, Kent
Ravensbourne Art College
Slade School of Art, London

Awards
D&AD Gold

Evening Standard, Best Advertisements
Paperchase, best Brochure
The London Group, Best New Artist selected by Albert Irvin RA

Solo and Group Exhibitions
1987 to present day-London and Paris

Associations past and present
Treasurer, Hon' Member National Society of Painters Sculptors & Printmakers
The Arts Club, Mayfair, London
Who's Who in Art
Beckenham Heritage Group (BHG) Known People

Currently living and working in Paris

Kindle epublishing on Amazon
Colours of Poetry, Number One. *17.12.2017*
Colours of Poetry II, Painting with words. *10.03.2020*
Colours of Poetry III, No Rhythm nor reason. *20.04.2020*
Tea & Poetry. The first 100 works from 'Colours of poetry'. *06.05.2020*
Colours of Poetry IV, Pros and cons. *22.05.2020*
Colours of Poetry V, Paradoxically seeking. *20.06.2020*
Colours of Poetry VI, Ambiguous parodies. *31.10.2020*
Coffee & Poetry, The Second 100 works from 'Colours of Poetry'. *24.12.20*
Colours of Poetry VII, And then some. *01.01.2020*
Colours of Poetry VIII, Affairs of the written word. *12.01.2021*
Colours of Poetry IX, Contemplate the now. *15.02.2021*

9 798710 071007